I WISH I WAS A BROWNIE

MARSHA CASPER COOK

PUBLISHED BY FIDELI PUBLISHING INC.

Copyright © 2015 by Marsha Casper Cook

I Wish I Was a Brownie
Paperback – published 2015 Fideli Publishing Inc.
ISBN: 978-1-60414-881-7

All rights reserved.

No part of this book may be reproduced or transmitted in any form or by any means, electronic or mechanical, including photocopying, recording, or by any information storage and retrieval system without the written permission of the author, except where permitted by law.

Illustrations by Mikey Brooks:
www.insidemikeysworld.com

To my Three Guys:

Stephen, Marcus and Myles, Thank you

And to all my friends - especially Bonnie - thank you for being there for me.

Once there was a chocolate chip cookie named Cliffy Chippy. Cliffy lived in Chippyville with his mom and dad, his three brothers, and his three sisters. Cliffy was the youngest Chippy. Everyone who lived in Chippyville was a chocolate chip cookie, except for Cliffy's dog, Rockwell. Rockwell was just a regular dog. You know, the kind that barks, licks your face, follows you everywhere, and is truly your best friend. That is Rockwell.

Instead of being happy, Cliffy was always sad. Cliffy didn't laugh or smile like the other Chippys. Cliffy never played with the other Chippys during school, or even after school. Never. After school, Cliffy would go straight home and play in his own yard. When it rained, he stayed inside all by himself. Sometimes, he felt so lonely that he would cry into his pillow so no one would hear him. Nobody ever did.

I Wish I Was a Brownie

One day at the Chippyville School, Cliffy's teacher, Mrs. Chipster, called on him during class. "Cliffy Chippy, will you please read page thirty to the class?"

Cliffy closed his eyes for a moment and thought. Right before he started to read, he took one last look around the room. Chocolate sweat fell from his brow. This time, Cliffy was very determined to read, but he couldn't. He froze. When he opened his mouth, the words just wouldn't come out. From the corner of Cliffy's eye, he could see the other Chippys giggling. Once again, Cliffy was embarrassed.

Mrs. Chipster became angry. She tapped her ruler on her desk to quiet the class. "Class, I think it might be a good time to have recess. I do hope this foolishness will stop when you return." Immediately, every Chippy sat upright in his or her seat. It was so quiet that you could hear a pin drop. Mrs. Chipster motioned to the class to line up. The Chippys lined up in single file at the door. All except Cliffy. He stayed at his desk. As soon as the last Chippy left the room, Cliffy rested his head on his desk and began to cry.

I Wish I Was a Brownie

A few minutes later, Mrs. Chipster returned to her classroom. She sat down at the seat next to Cliffy and handed him a tissue. "Cliffy, is there anything I can do to help you?"

Cliffy's eyes were sad as he answered. "I don't know."

Mrs. Chipster smiled in a very comforting way. "Cliffy, why don't you let me try? You don't have to worry. I won't laugh."

Cliffy bit down on his lip. Then, before fear could set in, the words flew right out of his mouth. "Sometimes I wish I was a brownie."

Mrs. Chipster stood up and placed her hand on Cliffy's shoulder. "I know exactly how you feel."

Cliffy seemed surprised. "You do?" he asked.

"Yes, I do," Mrs. Chipster said. "As a matter of fact, I was just about your age when being a brownie seemed so much more exciting."

Cliffy's eyes filled with hope. "Mrs. Chipster, do you really think you can help me?"

Mrs. Chipster nodded. "Yes, I do."

"Why don't you come over to my house after school? I'll check with your mom first."

"Can Rockwell come?" Cliffy asked.

A grin appeared on Mrs. Chipster's face. "Of course he can."

After school, Cliffy arrived at Mrs. Chipster's house with Rockwell at his side. They followed Mrs. Chipster into the kitchen. On the kitchen table was a large dish of ice cream for Chippy, and on the floor sat a small doggie dish filled with ice cream for Rockwell. Just as soon as Chippy and Rockwell were finished, they followed Mrs. Chipster up to the attic.

The attic was quite dusty. Chippy sneezed. "Ah...ah...ah...choo! Ah...ah...ah...choo!" Mrs. Chipster waved her hands back and forth to clear the air.

"I guess it's been longer than I thought since I've been up here," she said. "Cliffy, why don't you have a seat? There's something I'd like to show you." Cliffy sat in an old chair with Rockwell beside him. They both watched as Mrs. Chipster pulled out a large crate from behind a huge pile of books.

Time seemed to pass very slowly. Mrs. Chipster kept pulling out box after box, not finding what she had been looking for. Every time she opened a box that didn't have what she was looking for, she sighed. "Wheew," she said, "I know it's here."

Suddenly, with intense excitement, Mrs. Chipster shouted, "I found it!" Mrs. Chipster reached inside the crate and pulled out a red box. Inside the box was a costume.

"Cliffy, please try this on," she said.

Cliffy didn't have the slightest idea what any of this meant, but he did what Mrs. Chipster asked him to do. After all, she was his very favorite teacher.

While Cliffy was changing, Mrs. Chipster placed a full-length mirror in the center of the room.

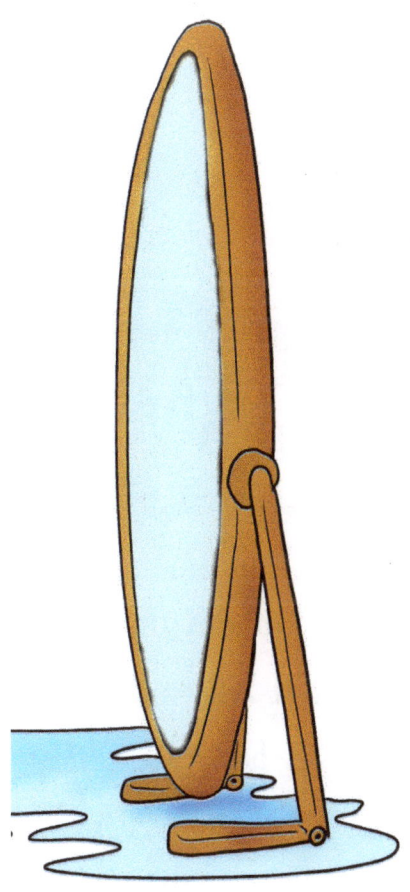

Cliffy's eyes were wide in amazement as he walked over to the mirror and saw what he looked like. He couldn't believe what he saw. Cliffy was a double, chocolate chip, nutty brownie with frosting. For a very long time, Cliffy stared into the mirror.

"How does it feel to be a brownie?" Mrs. Chipster asked.

Before answering, Cliffy took another look in the mirror.

"I still feel like me," Cliffy said. "I don't look like me, but inside I'm still me." Cliffy touched his lips with his fingers as he spoke. "Still sounds like me," he said.

Mrs. Chipster smiled as she walked over to Cliffy, who by now was as close to the mirror as he could possibly be.

Cliffy pressed his nose against the mirror. Then he moved back away from the mirror. When Cliffy waved into the mirror, the brownie waved back. Cliffy jumped

up and clapped his hands. The brownie did the same. Then, Cliffy did something he hadn't done in a very long time. He smiled. And, wouldn't you know it, the brownie did the same.

Then all of a sudden, Cliffy started to giggle and giggle and giggle. "I get it. It's me in the mirror, isn't it? I still feel like me, because it is me. I just look different. But on the inside, it's still me, Cliffy Chippy."

Mrs. Chipster laughed. "You're right. It is you, and that should always be enough."

"Do you really think so?" Cliffy asked.

Mrs. Chipster had been expecting Cliffy's question, and she answered him in the best way she knew how. "Cliffy, it's not really what we see in the mirror that's important. It's what we feel inside that makes all the difference. It's who we are and who we will grow up to be."

As Cliffy knelt down to hug Rockwell, he was met by wet sloppy kisses that felt great. "I can't even fool Rockwell," Cliffy said as he started taking off the brownie costume. "I don't think I'll be needing this brownie costume, Mrs. Chipster. Do you?"

"No, Cliffy," she answered. "I don't think so."

Cliffy and Rockwell were just about to walk out the door when Cliffy turned to Mrs. Chipster and asked, "What should I do when the other Chippys laugh at me?"

Mrs. Chipster looked at both Chippy and Rockwell and said, "Laugh right along with them. In no time at all, you and the other Chippys will be laughing together. That's what friends do." Cliffy nodded his head in approval, and Rockwell did the same.

Cliffy Chippy was now a happy chocolate chip cookie. He was happier than he had ever been. In fact, from what they say in Chippyville, Cliffy has quite a sense of humor. Instead of laughing at Cliffy the way they used to, now the other Chippys laugh at his jokes and the funny things he does.

The End

If you're wondering how this whole thing happened, here's a suggestion. Next time you look in the mirror, smile. If you want to, you can let your teeth show - you'll get a bigger smile that way.

The person - or cookie, as it may very well be - will smile back. It won't be Cliffy Chippy, but it will be you.

Give it a try.

It's fun.

You'll see.

Acknowledgments

Special Thank you to Robin Surface at Fideli Publishing, Jeff Fleischer my Editor, Mikey Brooks the Illustrator and Elyse M. Emmerling for narrating the audio book.

About the Author

Marsha Casper Cook was born and raised in Chicago. She is a Partner of the World of Ink Network, Agent, Award-winning Script Writer, Novelist, Writing Coach, Media Release Specialist, Blog Talk Radio Host and Founder of Michigan Avenue Media. Marsha Casper Cook is the author of 10 published books and 11 feature-length screenplays, a literary agent with 15 years of experience and the host of BTR's World of Ink Network shows: A Good Story Is a Good Story and special editions of The World of Ink Network. She and her guests discuss writing and what's new in the entertainment field. Marsha has also appeared as a guest on other network shows and will continue to make frequent visits to other shows.

Visit Marsha's website at
www.marshacaspercook.com

Other children's books by Marsha Casper Cook:

The Busy Bus

The Magical Leaping Lizard Potion

No Clues, No Shoes

Snack Attack

www.ingramcontent.com/pod-product-compliance
Lightning Source LLC
Chambersburg PA
CBHW061227070526
44584CB00029B/4022